Endpapers: Earth seen from space.

Kingfisher Books, Grisewood & Dempsey Ltd,
Elsley House, 24–30 Great Titchfield Street,
London W1P 7AD

First published in 1990 by Kingfisher Books

Copyright © Grisewood & Dempsey Ltd 1990

All rights reserved. No part of this publication may
be reproduced, stored in a retrieval system or
transmitted by any means, electronic, mechanical,
photocopying or otherwise, without the prior permission
of the publisher.

BRITISH LIBRARY CATALOGUING IN PUBLICATION DATA
Kramer, Ann
  Revolution and technology.
  1. Technological change. Social aspects
  I. Title   II. Adams, Simon III. Series
  306'.46

ISBN 0-86272-436-8

Editors: Nicola Barber and Annabel Warburg
Series editor: Ann Kramer
Series designer: Robert Wheeler
Cover design: Terry Woodley
Maps: Eugene Fleury and Malcolm Porter
Illustrations: Kevin Maddison and Stephen Conlin
Picture research: Elaine Willis
Phototypeset by Rowland Phototypesetting Ltd, Bury St Edmunds, Suffolk
Printed in Spain

HISTORICAL ATLAS

REVOLUTION & TECHNOLOGY

Rapid Change and the Growth of the Modern World

Ann Kramer & Simon Adams

KINGFISHER BOOKS

Contents

The World in 1760 and After
1760–1815
page 8

The world in 1760 *8, 9* ■ The Industrial Revolution *10, 11* ■ The American Revolution *12* ■ **THE FRENCH REVOLUTION** *13* ■ Napoleonic Europe *14* ■ South America *15* ■

Imperialism and Empire
1880–1914
page 22

Empire-builders *22, 23* ■ China and Japan *24, 25* ■ A changing world *26* ■ **TRANSPORT** *27* ■

The Impact of Revolution
1815–1880
page 16

Industrial nations *16, 17* ■ Europe after 1815 *18* ■ **SCIENCE** *19* ■ The growth of the United States *20, 21* ■

The World at War
1914–1945
page 28

The First World War *28* ■ **THE RUSSIAN REVOLUTION** *29* ■ The aftermath of war *30, 31* ■ The Second World War *32, 33* ■

A Troubled World
1945–   *page 34*
The Cold War *34, 35* ■ China *36* ■
TECHNOLOGY AND POP CULTURE
37 ■ A divided world *38, 39* ■
One World? *40* ■

Glossary   *page 41*

Timeline   *pages 42, 43*

Index   *pages 44, 45*

Introduction

This book tells the story of the world from 1760 to the present day. During those years, the world changed faster than ever before. Great empires came and went. Two world wars and many smaller ones were fought. The United States, France, Russia and China experienced political revolutions that also affected the rest of the world. An industrial and scientific revolution transformed the way we live today.

But history is not just about dates and events. It is about people and how they lived in the past. Using illustrations, maps and photographs, *Revolution & Technology* takes a close look at the daily lives of people during this period and the discoveries and inventions they made. Feature boxes examine the impact of the French and Russian revolutions, the development of science and transport one hundred years ago, and the technological revolution still happening today.

Revolution & Technology is divided into five chapters. The first shows the world as it was in 1760. The following chapters tell the history of different periods and different regions of the world, with maps to show where the events took place. Difficult words in the text are highlighted in **bold** and are explained in a glossary on page 41, while a Timeline on pages 42 and 43 provides a list of key dates.

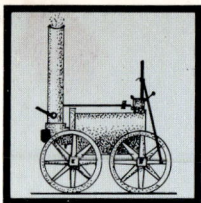

The World in 1760 and After

The world in 1760

In 1760 much of the world was dominated by Europe. Ever since the Genoese explorer Christopher Columbus had sailed across the Atlantic Ocean to the Caribbean in 1492, European merchants and sailors had been exploring the world. They had founded **colonies** and established **trading** links in every part of the world.

By 1760, Britain was the most powerful colonial and trading power in the world. Britain ruled large **empires** in North America and India. The British navy dominated the seas and Britain had established an extensive overseas trading network. France too was a wealthy and powerful **nation**, with colonies in the Caribbean. Spain and Portugal governed most of Central and South America, and, like the Netherlands, had colonies and trading posts in Africa and the Far East. In Asia, the Russians governed a huge empire that stretched from eastern Europe to the Pacific Ocean, while the Ottoman Turks ruled over much of eastern Europe, the Middle East and north Africa.

However, most of Africa and the wealthy empires of China and Japan remained independent of European control, although China and Japan had limited trade with Europe.

▶ In 1760 there were few parts of the world that were not under European control. North and South America, the coast of Africa, India and much of the Far East were governed from Europe and from them merchants sent back valuable cargoes to make Europe the wealthiest part of the world.

(page 9, bottom left) A British merchant ship known as an East Indiaman, in Calcutta, India.

(page 9, bottom right) Ambassadors at the Meridian Gate, Peking in China. There were four cities at Peking, each surrounded by great walls. China was only prepared to have limited trade with Europe.

◀ In many parts of the world the European rulers enslaved the local population and made them work on sugar, tea and other plantations.

1760

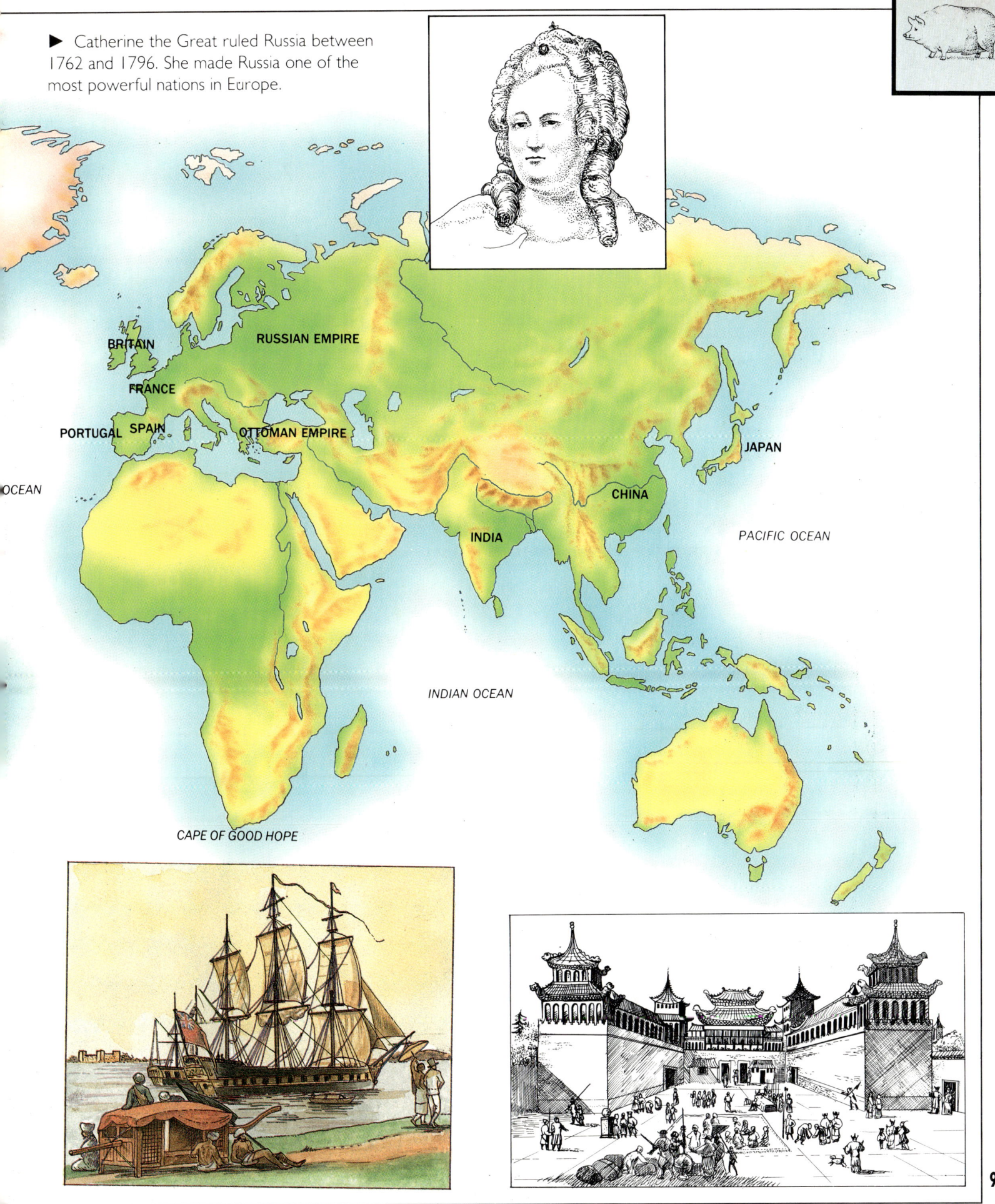

► Catherine the Great ruled Russia between 1762 and 1796. She made Russia one of the most powerful nations in Europe.

1760

The Industrial Revolution

During the 1700s, Europe experienced a number of important social and **economic** changes whose effects remain today. The population of Europe doubled during the 1700s, and people began to move from the countryside to the cities. By 1800, Paris and London each contained more than one million inhabitants and other European cities were growing fast. To feed this rising population new agricultural techniques were developed.

The biggest changes took place in industry where Britain, followed by other countries, underwent what is known as the Industrial Revolution. Starting in Britain in about 1760, the Industrial Revolution transformed the way in which goods were produced. Machinery was developed that was powered by coal and water. Inventions such as the steam engine and steam pump, the blast furnace, and the spinning jenny revolutionized the manufacture of goods, particularly textiles. Methods of working changed too. Previously, most textiles had been produced in people's homes in 'cottage industries'. Now the new machines were built in factories where many workers – men, women and children – worked together under one roof.

As a result, British manufacturers could produce more goods than their foreign competitors. By 1815 Britain led world trade and was 'the workshop of the world'.

Heavy goods such as coal or iron were slow and expensive to move by road. Canals provided a cheaper alternative and by 1830, 4,000 km (2,500 miles) of canals had been built in Britain.

▲ After 1760, Britain became the industrial centre of the world. The country possessed plentiful supplies of coal and iron ore. A large network of roads, navigable rivers and canals was created to transport these raw materials to new industrial towns. There they were made into manufactured goods, notably textiles and ironware, and exported around the world.

△ Cotton
○ Wool
◇ Iron

The Agricultural Revolution

During the 1700s, Britain experienced an Agricultural Revolution. Farmers enclosed the old open, mixed fields of crops and pasture, and used new and intensive methods of farming. This increased food production but also drove farmworkers off the land and into the towns.

1760–1815

▶ Water power had been used for centuries to drive machines and so the first factories of the Industrial Revolution were all situated near a supply of running water, usually in hilly areas. After 1768, the development of the coal-fired steam engine meant that factories could be built wherever there was a good supply of coal.

▼ The British engineer, Thomas Newcomen, built the first steam engine in 1709 but it was only used for land drainage. In 1768, James Watt improved the original design and adapted it to drive factory machines.

▼ During the Agricultural Revolution, farmers began to experiment with new breeds of pig and other livestock. Larger pigs such as this Berkshire hog, and new breeds of sheep, produced twice as much meat as before. Improved cows led to an increase in dairy products.

◀ In 1764, James Hargreaves invented the spinning jenny – a machine that could spin up to 100 threads of cotton at one time. Previously, cotton was spun by hand, one thread at a time, by workers in their homes. The jenny replaced this domestic industry with workers who were employed in factories.

▶ The development of factories was seen as a threat to the jobs and independence of craftworkers. After 1810, a group of workers, known as Luddites, smashed machines in protest at their new working conditions. This cartoon shows the Luddite leader disguised as a woman.

1760–1815

The American Revolution

Towards the end of the 1700s two revolutions occurred: the first in North America and the second in France. In both of them, people demanded **democratic** government and rights for the individual.

In 1763, Britain had defeated France to become the major colonial power in North America. But after the war, relations between Britain and its 13 colonies on the North Atlantic coast began to deteriorate. The immediate cause of these problems was **taxation**. The colonists made their own local laws but their finances and trade were controlled by the British government. Increasingly, the colonists resented paying taxes to a government in which they were not represented and which they did not elect or choose.

In 1774, the 13 **states** came together in a Continental Congress to discuss their relations with Britain. But revolution broke out in 1775 when shots were exchanged between colonists and the British army at Lexington. In 1776, Congress declared that the 13 colonies were **independent** of Britain, and by 1781 the American forces had defeated the British army. In 1783, the British recognized the independence of their former colonies. The rebels had won and they set up a new, united, nation – the United States of America. In 1789, George Washington became first president of the new nation.

▲ In 1774, a group of women colonists in Edenton, North Carolina protested against a British tax on tea by refusing to drink tea. The previous year, colonists in Boston threw £18,000 worth of tea into the harbour in a similar protest, now known as the Boston Tea Party.

▼ Signing the Declaration of Independence, issued in 1776 by the Continental Congress. Drawn up by Thomas Jefferson, the document declared that 'all men are created equal' and that they have the right to 'Life, Liberty and the Pursuit of Happiness'. Ideas such as these had a strong influence on later revolutionary movements.

1760–1815

The French Revolution

By 1789, French society was already deeply divided, for the middle classes resented the power of the king, the **aristocracy** and the Church. The people were heavily taxed, and many of them were starving. In 1789, King Louis XIV summoned the French parliament, to raise more taxes. Almost immediately, the **bourgeoisie**, the middle-class representatives, challenged the power of the king and set up a National Assembly to rule France. Riots broke out and the people of Paris stormed the royal fortress of the Bastille. The Revolution then quickly spread throughout the country. In 1792 the National Convention, which had replaced the Assembly, deposed the king and declared France a **republic**. Power passed to a political group known as the Girondins. In 1793 they executed the king for treason. Later the same year, a more radical group of politicians known as the Jacobins took power under Maximilien Robespierre. Their reign of terror lasted until 1794, during which they executed all those suspected of opposing the Revolution. In 1799 the Revolution ended when Napoleon Bonaparte seized power.

◀ The Tricolour, the new flag of Republican France.

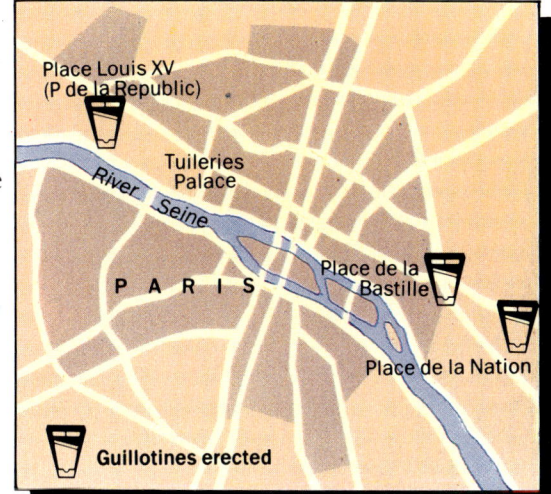

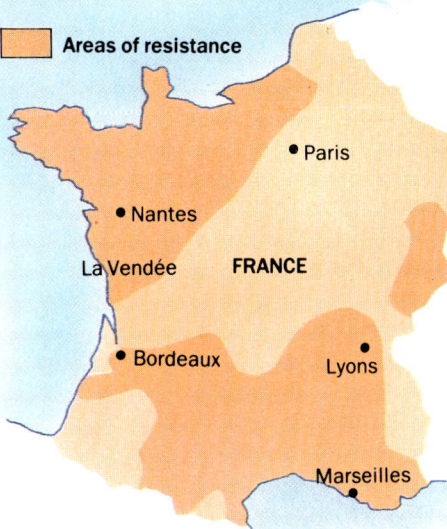

◀ The French Revolution began in Paris when the citizens stormed the Bastille Fortress in 1789. But it soon spread to the rest of the country. Some areas stayed loyal to the king; in the Vendée region of western France, a royalist revolt in 1793 was put down with considerable ferocity.

▼ Women led many of the marches and demonstrations during the French Revolution, demanding greater freedom and enough food to feed their families. Many suffered from starvation during the bad harvests. Despite their part in the Revolution, women were never allowed to vote or participate in the government.

▲ The guillotine quickly became the symbol of the Revolution. It was used to execute aristocrats and other opponents of the Revolution. More than 40,000 men and women were guillotined between 1789 and 1794.

Napoleonic Europe

The American colonies won their independence from Britain in 1783, with considerable French support. France had wanted revenge for the loss of its American colonies to Britain in 1763. But the American Revolution inspired people in France to seek their own freedom, and in 1789 a revolution broke out in France itself (page 13).

By 1793 all Europe was involved in the French Revolution. An alliance of European states was formed against France but France had an army of more than 750,000 – the biggest in Europe – and by 1797 France had defeated all its enemies except Britain. This success was due to the quality of the French commanders, particularly Napoleon Bonaparte, who, in 1796, at the age of 26, had taken command of the army. In 1799 he seized control of the French government and in 1804 he crowned himself Emperor of the French.

Napoleon reorganized the law, administration, education and economy of France. His army was unbeatable, and by 1812 he had conquered most of Europe. But his attempts to conquer Spain met with great resistance. In 1812 he unsuccessfully invaded Russia and his army suffered heavy losses retreating from Moscow. In 1815 Napoleon was finally defeated by the British and their allies at Waterloo. He was sent into exile on the South Atlantic island of St Helena, where he died in 1821.

▲ In 1812, Napoleon and his family ruled an empire that dominated Europe. He reorganized Germany and Italy into allied states, and Prussia and Austria were considerably reduced in size and power. Only Britain remained independent. But the French Empire was weakened by the wars against Spain and Russia, and was finally overthrown in 1815.

▶ Napoleon was a military genius who had conquered most of Europe by 1812. His empire did not survive him, but many of his administrative and educational reforms are still in force in France today.

◀ A plate from a dinner service made for Napoleon. In 1798, Napoleon led a French army to Egypt to cut British trade links with India. While in Egypt, French archaeologists excavated the ancient Sphinx, which had been buried in the desert sand for hundreds of years and investigated the Pyramids.

◀ In 1808, Napoleon invaded Spain and placed his brother on the throne. Although the French introduced many reforms, their rule was not popular and the Spanish people revolted. Many civilians were killed, as this painting by Francisco Goya shows.

▼ The dates of independence of the European colonies in South America.

▲ The French controlled the Caribbean island of Haiti, the richest colony in the world. Its wealth was created by the many slaves who worked on its **plantations**. In 1801, the slaves, led by Toussaint l'Ouverture, rose in revolt. L'Ouverture was captured and killed by the French in 1803, but in 1804 Haiti became an independent country.

▼ José de San Martin, (left) liberator of Argentina and Chile. He led his army across the Andes mountains, a military achievement.

▲ In 1808 Napoleon made his brother Joseph king of Spain. The Spanish colonies in South America refused to accept their new ruler and declared their independence. Led by Simon Bolívar (above) and José de San Martin, all the former Spanish territories became independent by 1825.

1760–1815

The Impact of Revolution

Industrial nations

The upheavals caused by the Industrial and French Revolutions affected every aspect of social and political life for the next 100 years.

Although the Industrial Revolution began in Britain, the new **technologies** and methods of production soon spread to Belgium, France, Germany and Italy. At first, Britain was strong enough to fight off any competition. In 1850, one-quarter of all the world's trade passed through British ports and over one-third of the world's industrial output was British. The first railway was tested in the north of England in 1825 and the first passenger train operated between Liverpool and Manchester in 1830. The railway revolutionized communications, and by 1870 there were 25,000 km (15,500 miles) of railway track in Britain alone.

Other countries soon began to challenge British industrial and economic supremacy. After 1870, new steel and chemical industries were established in Germany, while by 1900 the United States had become the most powerful industrial nation in the world, with vast steel, oil and food production industries. Russia, too, developed an iron and steel industry and Japan started to build up an industrial economy.

▲ The Industrial Revolution began in Britain but soon spread throughout Europe. Mines and factories opened up near supplies of coal and iron and new towns were built to accommodate the expanding workforce. Across Europe, the population increased dramatically as the new factories required more workers.

○ **Coalfields**
◇ **Iron ore fields**
□ **Textile industry**

▶ Men, women and children worked long hours for low pay in the mines and factories of industrial Britain. In the early coal mines men hacked the coal out of the seams and women then dragged it or carried it along the narrow tunnels. From the 1830s, however, laws were introduced to improve working conditions.

1815–1880

▲ Until the 1850s, steel was expensive to produce, costing almost 20 times as much as iron. In 1856, Henry Bessemer, an English engineer, developed a cheap way of producing steel and within a few years steel had replaced iron in the construction of railways, ships, machinery and buildings. This factory, in the Ruhr valley in West Germany, made weapons from steel.

◀ In 1851, Britain held an international exhibition in London to show off the industrial and manufacturing might of the country. The Great Exhibition was housed in a remarkable iron and glass building, called the Crystal Palace; it was erected in only seven months.

▲ The Industrial Revolution created many new towns and enlarged many old ones, but conditions in the towns were overcrowded and poor. Many of the houses were badly built and had no running water or sewage disposal and they quickly became slums. Disease and poverty were common in all major cities.

▶ Poor children were sent to work in factories or even mines as soon as they were old enough to walk and talk. They received little formal education and were made to work long hours for little pay. Child labour was common in European and American factories until well into the 20th century.

1815–1880

Europe after 1815

After Napoleon's defeat in 1815, the victorious allies met in Vienna to redraw the map of Europe. The French monarchy was restored, and Austria became dominant in central Europe. Throughout Europe, aristocratic government was restored and Napoleon's reforms were reversed everywhere except in France.

The Vienna settlement lasted only a few years. The French Revolution had introduced to Europe two ideas: democracy, in which the people had a say in the government and **nationalism**, in which people speaking a common language and living together in one country or region had the right to rule themselves. However, the 1815 settlement left many peoples under undemocratic, foreign control, and major uprisings soon occurred. In 1821, the Greeks revolted against their Turkish rulers and won independence in 1829, and in 1830 the Belgians overthrew Dutch rule.

In 1848 revolutions occurred throughout Europe. The monarchy was again overthrown in France and nationalists revolted against Austrian rule in Italy, Germany and Hungary. By 1851 the revolts had been crushed. But nationalism remained strong in Italy and Germany. Led by Count Cavour, the various Italian states drove out the Austrians by 1866 and Italy was united by 1870. In 1871, all Germany was united under the powerful rule of Prussia.

▲ In Britain, the Chartists – a mass movement of men and women – demanded political reform and the right to vote. Between 1838 and 1848 they held vast demonstrations and presented a series of petitions to Parliament.

▶ In 1848, the German thinker Karl Marx wrote the *Communist Manifesto* urging workers to overthrow undemocratic governments. At the time, the book was not widely read, but during the 20th century, Marx's ideas have strongly influenced modern revolutionary movements in Russia, China and South America.

▼ In 1848, many countries in Europe erupted in revolution.

1815–1880

Science

▲ This contemporary cartoon attacks the British biologist Charles Darwin, who, in 1859, published *The Origin of Species*. In this book he proposed that over many thousands of years humans had evolved from apes.

▲ A picture taken during the American Civil War, the first war to be recorded by photograph. In 1839, the Frenchman Louis Daguerre produced the first successful photograph. Only one photograph could be produced at a time.

▼ In 1861 the French chemist Louis Pasteur discovered that diseases do not occur by themselves but are the result of germs carried in the air. This discovery led him to develop pasteurization, a method of sterilizing (cleaning) milk.

During the 1800s, science and medicine were revolutionized, as a series of remarkable developments transformed the way in which people lived and thought about the world around them. Scientists such as Louis Pasteur discovered the cause of diseases; doctors such as Joseph Lister introduced effective antiseptics for the prevention of infections; and, for the first time, the workings of the human mind were scientifically investigated when the Austrian doctor, Sigmund Freud, began his investigations into mental illness at the end of the century. In 1859, the British biologist Charles Darwin shocked the Western world when he suggested that human life had begun, not with their creation by God, but through a long process of evolution from the apes. Throughout the 1800s, there was a constant stream of new technological developments.

▲ In the 1890s, the Frenchwoman Marie Curie investigated uranium, which is now used to produce nuclear power.

▲ In the late 1800s and early 1900s, Sigmund Freud studied human behaviour by interpreting dreams.

19

The growth of the United States

When the United States of America became independent from Britain in 1783, it consisted of only the 13 original British colonies on the Atlantic east coast. But it grew quickly after independence, and in little more than 80 years had trebled in size, reaching right across to the Pacific Ocean, and up to the Arctic Circle in the north.

In 1803, France sold the land to the west of the Mississippi River for $15 million, which doubled the size of the country. By 1867, gains from Spain, Britain, Mexico and Russia gave the country its present shape. But throughout the 1800s there were fierce battles for control between the European settlers and the native Americans, or American Indians, who had lived there for thousands of years. Though brave, the American Indians had little defence against American troops, and by 1890 the Indians had been overcome and confined to reservations.

Between 1803 and 1900, the population of the United States rose from four million to 90 million. Many of these people were immigrants fleeing from poverty and oppression in Europe. They spoke many different languages and brought many skills to their new country. Some prospered, others remained poor, but a rich and strong nation emerged. By 1900, the United States was the world's most powerful industrial and **commercial** nation.

▲ By 1848, the original 13 American colonies on the Atlantic coast had expanded across the continent to the Pacific Ocean. It was many years later before these vast tracts of land were fully settled by farmers and their families, who moved slowly westwards from the crowded eastern states.

▼ In 1828 the first railway line was opened in America and by 1869 the two sides of the continent were connected by 85,000 km (52,000 miles) of railway. The railway did much to open up the West and to create a truly united country.

1815–1880

◀ The early North American settlers lived hard lives. They had to defend their lands against the local Indians and they were always at the mercy of bad weather or harvest failure. The settlers built homes of turf or even soil and it was years before they could afford to build secure wooden houses.

▼ In 1861, **civil war** broke out in America between the southern states, who wished to keep slaves on their plantations, and the northern states, who wished to abolish **slavery**. The northern states won the war with great brutality in 1865, but the south was devastated. This picture shows a New York ferry, converted into a gunboat for use by the northern states.

▶ Sitting Bull was chief of the Sioux tribe and one of the most famous of Indian leaders. In 1876 he killed General Custer at the Battle of the Little Big Horn and continued to fight for the rights of the Indian peoples until his death in 1890.

▶ Harriet Tubman was an escaped slave who spent much of her life fighting slavery. During the Civil War she organized an escape network known as the Underground Railway, through which more than 300 slaves escaped to freedom.

21

1815–1880

Imperialism and Empire

Empire-builders

In 1880, most of Africa consisted of independent nations. Their economies were based on agriculture, and they traded with other African countries. Contact with Europe was limited, although the British, French and Portuguese maintained small colonial trading posts on the coast, while the Ottoman Empire had loose control of north-eastern Africa. By 1914, with the exception of the independent states of Ethiopia and Liberia, every part of Africa was controlled by Europeans. Africa's economy had been transformed to provide raw materials for European industries.

Similarly the British had established complete control of India and its neighbours, and of Australia and New Zealand, while much of the Far East was ruled by other European powers. The main reason for this expansion overseas was that, by 1880, the Industrial Revolution had spread across Europe. The new industries needed cheap supplies of raw materials, and this led European nations to exploit the vast and untapped resources of Africa and the Far East. By 1914 Britain had built up the world's biggest empire. It covered one-quarter of the world's land surface and included one-quarter of its population. France, Belgium,

continues on page 24

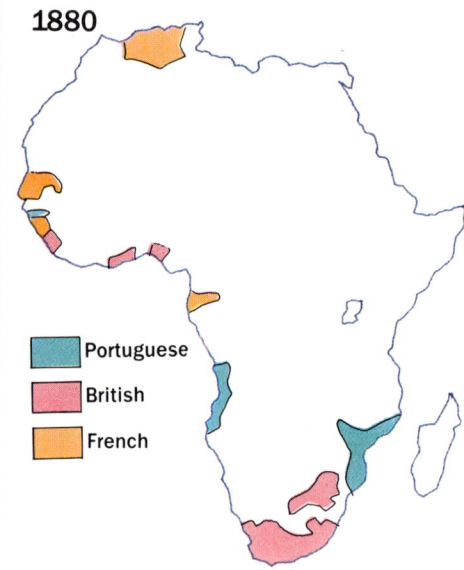

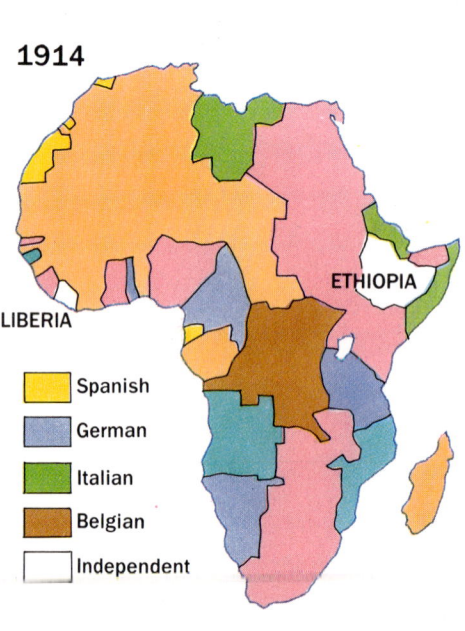

▲ In 1880, most of Africa consisted of independent nations, with only the Ottoman Empire ruling any significant territory in Africa. By 1914, the continent had been carved up by Europeans and only two nations remained independent of foreign control.

▲ The Englishwoman Mary Kingsley was an enterprising explorer who travelled throughout West Africa in the late 1800s. Many of the people she encountered had never met a European woman before.

▼ Cecil Rhodes was Prime Minister of the British-controlled Cape Colony in South Africa. He dreamed of building a railway from the Cape in the south to Cairo in the north that would run entirely through British territory.

1880–1914

▲ In 1869, the Suez Canal was opened connecting the Mediterranean Sea to the Indian Ocean. Because of its strategic position on the route from Britain to its empire in India, it was acquired by Britain in 1875.

▲ British influence in India was considerable. Many of the British people living in India preserved as much as possible their British customs and ways of life. Here two Englishmen take afternoon tea, attended by their Indian servants.

▼ Southern Africa is rich in gold and diamonds. During the late 1800s a number of powerful mining companies were set up, controlled by Europeans and using slave labour.

European Settlement of South Africa

The first European settlers in South Africa were the Dutch, who established a colony on the Cape of Good Hope in 1652. The British took over the colony in 1814 and in 1833 abolished the slavery of black Africans on the farms and plantations. This angered the Boers, as the original Dutch settlers were known, and in 1835 they trekked inland to form two new independent republics. Continual conflicts between the Boers and the British led to war in 1899. By 1902 the British had won, and in 1910 the country was united and became an independent state known as the Union of South Africa.

1880–1914

continued from page 22

Portugal, Spain, Italy and the newly-united Germany all established colonies in Africa. Meanwhile the United States acquired territory in the Caribbean and the Far East. By 1914 the United States and eight European nations controlled eighty-five per cent of the world's land surface.

China and Japan

Until the mid-1800s, very few Europeans had been allowed into the empires of China or Japan. The Chinese in particular had a hatred of foreigners and allowed them to trade only in certain areas. Britain, however, was keen to extend its influence. In 1839, it went to war with China, and in 1842 the Chinese were forced to sign a treaty surrendering Hong Kong and allowing Britain to trade in other ports. Within China, revolts against the Ch'in **Dynasty** weakened the empire, allowing European influence to increase. The Chinese government's failure to resist the Europeans in turn led to further rebellions and in 1911 a revolution finally overthrew the empire and established a republic.

Japan had almost no trading contact with foreigners until 1853, when an American naval squadron sailed to Japan and forced the Japanese to trade with the United States. Europeans followed and Japan made trade agreements with many countries. Over the years, Japan developed railways and factories and by 1905 had become a major industrial nation.

▲ By 1905 Britain, France and Russia dominated much of China and Japan had gained an empire of its own in Korea and Taiwan.

▶ In 1900 a Chinese secret society known as the 'Boxers' rebelled against Western intervention, attacking railways, factories and European embassies. The rebellion was put down by European and Japanese armies, who established control over much of the country. This Chinese cartoon attacks Westerners.

▼ In the 1850s the waterfront of the Chinese city of Canton was full of Europeans but they were not allowed into the interior of China for many years.

24

1880–1914

▲ In 1872 the first railway line was completed in Japan by British engineers. Within 30 years, more than 8000 km (5000 miles) of track had been laid and Japan had become one of the most powerful industrial states in the world.

▲ In 1853 and 1854 the American naval commander Matthew Perry visited Japan and forced the government to grant trading concessions to American shipping. It was the first Japanese contact with foreigners for more than 200 years.

▼ In their rush to modernize their country, many Japanese people, including the royal family, gave up their traditional costumes in favour of Western clothes.

1880-1914

A changing world

In the years immediately after 1900 wars broke out in Europe, Africa and the Far East, and there was internal unrest in many industrial nations. Much of the trouble was caused by the fact that the European powers were competing against each other to control trade and to increase their empires. By 1900 Germany had become the major industrial power in Europe, and this led to considerable rivalry with the established industrial nations such as Britain. An **arms race** developed between the European powers. Britain, France and Russia formed an **alliance** to protect themselves against Germany, while Germany allied itself with Austria.

There was also considerable social unrest in many countries. In 1905 revolution broke out in Russia against the autocratic rule of the Tsar. Although unsuccessful, the revolution seriously weakened the country. In 1912 war broke out in eastern Europe as the local peoples fought to overthrow their Turkish rulers and prevent Austria from taking over. This fighting increased tension throughout Europe, which found itself divided into two heavily armed camps. In Ireland there was almost civil war by 1914, caused by the demands of the Irish for self-government, while throughout Europe poor wages and bad working conditions led to much social unrest. By 1914 the whole continent was in turmoil.

▼ A dole queue in Britain. During the late 1800s governments began to take responsibility for the welfare of their people. Many countries introduced compulsory education, and pensions were provided for the old. State insurance was introduced to protect workers against unemployment or sickness and workers received 'dole' money if they lost their jobs.

◀ Elected parliaments were the most common form of government in Europe and the United States. By 1900 working men had gained the vote in most countries but women were not allowed to vote at all, except in New Zealand, which in 1893 became the first country to give women the vote. The United States followed in 1920, but it was not until 1928, after many years of struggle, that all British women over 21 were allowed to vote.

▼ In the years leading up to 1914 there was an arms race in Europe between the major powers. Weapons such as this German howitzer were capable of great destruction.

1880–1914

Transport

Throughout the 1800s new forms of transport revolutionized communications throughout the world. Railways, steamships, motor cars, bicycles and, in the early years of the 1900s, airships and aircraft, all increased the speed and efficiency of human travel. An organized tourist industry started to grow up, and people began to visit foreign countries in large numbers. Trade between different countries became easier and cheaper, while refrigeration enabled perishable foodstuffs to be transported around the world. As a result of these developments all parts of the world were linked together as never before.

▼ The development of the bicycle in the mid-1800s offered a cheap form of transport and recreation to large numbers of people.

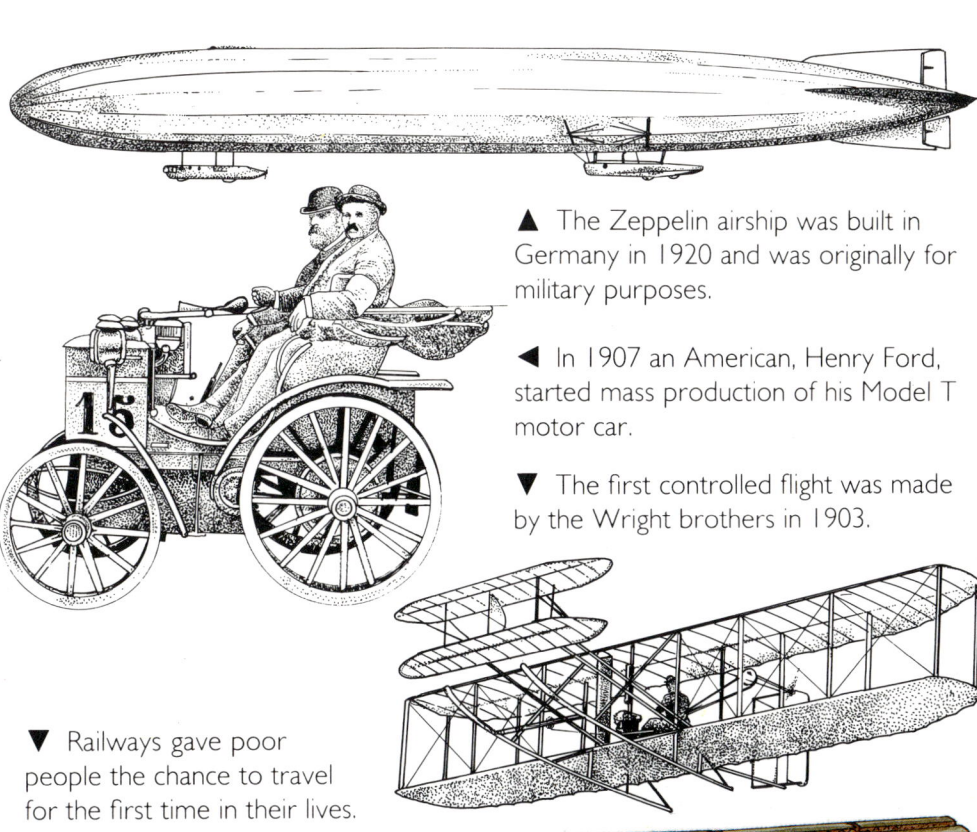

▲ The Zeppelin airship was built in Germany in 1920 and was originally for military purposes.

◀ In 1907 an American, Henry Ford, started mass production of his Model T motor car.

▼ The first controlled flight was made by the Wright brothers in 1903.

▼ Railways gave poor people the chance to travel for the first time in their lives.

▼ In 1882 the refrigerator ship *Dunedin* brought frozen meat from New Zealand to Europe.

The World at War

The First World War

In 1914 war broke out in Europe, lasting for four years and involving the whole world. The immediate cause of the war was the assassination of the heir to the Austrian throne in June 1914. Austria blamed its neighbour and enemy Serbia for the murder and declared war on it; soon all Europe was at war. Few nations remained **neutral** and fighting extended overseas for control of Germany's African and Far Eastern colonies, and for Turkish territories in the Middle East.

Between France and Germany a line of defensive trenches stretched along the Western Front, where millions of soldiers were killed. In eastern Europe, the war was equally savage. For three years there was stalemate, but in 1917 the Russian Revolution forced Russia to leave the war. In an effort to starve Britain and France into surrender, Germany attacked their supply ships in the Atlantic. Some American ships were sunk, and in 1917 the United States declared war on Germany. The vast numbers of American troops proved decisive, and in November 1918 the war ended. Of the 65 million men who fought in the war 10 million died, and more than 20 million were injured. It was the bloodiest war in human history.

▲ Most soldiers in the First World War spent their time in damp and dangerous trenches on the Western Front, being bombarded by enemy shells.

▶ For the first time in history, whole populations were involved in war. Many women worked, producing armaments and keeping industry going while the men were in the army.

▼ The First World War split Europe into two armed camps.

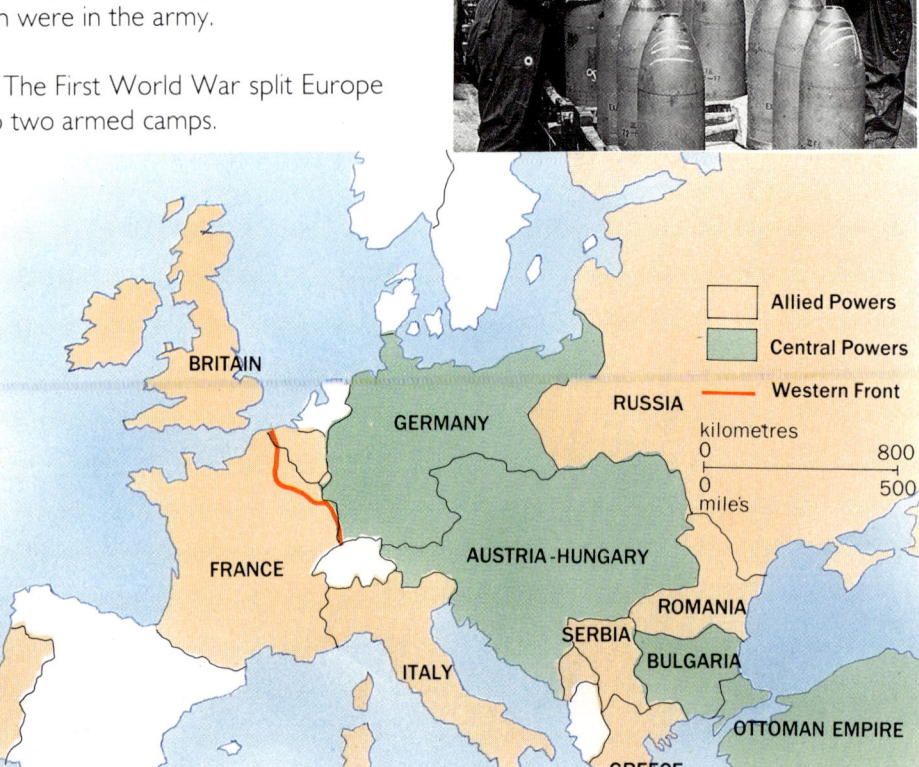

28

1914–1945

The Russian Revolution

In 1917 a revolution took place in Russia that was to change the course of modern history. The revolution occurred because many people suffered poverty and hardship. The government of Nicholas the Second was brutal but inefficient and it fought the war against Germany very incompetently.

In February 1917 a **general strike** broke out in Petrograd (as St Petersburg was then known; today the city is called Leningrad) in protest against the conduct of the war and the economic chaos at home. The army joined the strike and Nicholas was forced to abdicate his throne. A provisional government was formed but it had little support and in October 1917 the Communists (or Bolsheviks, as they were known) seized power. Led by

Vladimir Ilyich Illyanov (Lenin)

Lenin (*left*), the Bolsheviks quickly took control of the country and declared a Soviet republic, known today as the Soviet Union. The Bolsheviks made peace with Germany. The large estates were broken up and given to the peasants, banks were taken into state control and workers were given control of their factories. The world's first communist state had been founded.

▲ Four-fifths of the Russian population were peasants. Some of them found work hauling barges down the River Volga.

▶ In 1924 Joseph Stalin succeeded Lenin as head of the Soviet Union. He took all the land into state ownership and forced the peasants to work on the new collective farms. This is a poster advertising collectivism.

◀ Alexandra Kollontai was the only woman in the Bolshevik government. She was committed to economic change and to equality between women and men.

The aftermath of war

In 1919, the 30 states involved in the First World War met at Versailles in France, to draw up a peace settlement. Four empires – Germany, Austria, Russia and Turkey – had collapsed and many countries wanted independence. The map of Europe was redrawn and some new countries came into existence. The League of Nations was set up to work for peaceful settlements rather than war, but few countries obeyed its instructions.

The Versailles settlement was soon in trouble. The German economy collapsed because of the reparations (payments) Germany was forced to make for its part in the war. Other nations suffered from the heavy repayments they had to make to the United States for money borrowed during the war. The result was considerable political and economic upheaval. In 1929, an economic crisis, known as the Great Depression began.

Millions of people were thrown out of work. During the 1930s there was widespread unemployment and social unrest in Europe and in the United States. The president of the United States, Franklin Roosevelt helped the poor and unemployed through a programme of government aid known as the New Deal. In Germany, however, an extreme nationalist, Adolf Hitler, came to power in 1933. He promised to set unemployed Germans to work by restoring German power in Europe.

► The Treaty of Versailles in 1919 broke up the German, Austrian and Russian empires and replaced them with new states throughout Eastern Europe. Germany became smaller and was split into two parts. Poland and Finland re-emerged as independent nations. The Austro–Hungarian Empire was split into four new countries, with parts of it also going to Italy, Poland and Romania. Three new states were created on the Baltic.

◄ During the early 1900s, the first films appeared. They were in black and white and had no sound. By 1930, films were in colour and had sound. Many films were produced in Hollywood, California, known as the film capital of the world.

▼ In 1929, the value of shares on the American Stock Exchange on Wall Street crashed as investors lost confidence in the American economy. Banks failed and an economic depression began that soon spread throughout the world.

1914–1945

▲ India remained a British colony after 1919. But demands for independence grew, led by the Indian nationalist Mahatma Gandhi.

▲ The Depression caused terrible suffering to American farmers. Prices fell and drought affected the crops. Whole families were forced to leave their farms in the mid-west to look for other work in California.

▼ **Fascism** was carried to extremes by Hitler, leader of the Nazi party, who was named the German Chancellor in 1933. Economic, cultural and religious life were all brought under central government control. Here Hitler leads a military parade in honour of his birthday in 1941.

▼ In 1936, Civil War broke out in Spain between the Republican Government and the Fascists led by General Franco. Helped by Italy and Germany, Franco defeated the government in a brutal war. He ruled Spain as **dictator** from 1939 to 1975. This poster shows a soldier off to fight against the Fascists saying to his baby: 'I Go to Fight for Your Future'.

31

1914–1945

The Second World War

When Hitler became the leader of Germany in 1933, he created a German empire in Central Europe. By 1939 he had seized Austria and Czechoslovakia. Most European nations were anxious to avoid the horrors of another war, but when in 1939 Hitler invaded Poland, Britain and France declared war on Germany. Italy joined the war on the German side.

For six years, war raged in Europe, North Africa, Russia and the Pacific. Continual air raids destroyed many cities. By 1941, Germany had conquered most of Europe, except for Britain, and had advanced into Russia. In the Far East, Japan allied with Germany and invaded China, Burma and other parts of South East Asia.

In December 1941, Japanese planes bombed the American naval base at Pearl Harbor, in Hawaii. The United States sided with Britain and together they reconquered North Africa, invaded Italy, and, in 1944, liberated France from German control. As American and British troops advanced on Germany from the west, Russian troops advanced from the east. As they neared Berlin in April 1945, Hitler committed suicide and the war in Europe ended. In August the Americans dropped the first atomic bomb on the Japanese city of Hiroshima and a second on Nagasaki, and Japan surrendered.

It was a brutal end to a brutal war. Fifty million people had been killed or injured and another 43 million wounded. Europe was devastated.

▲ War touched every part of the globe as soldiers from all over the British Empire fought the war on Britain's side.

▲ One of Hitler's most dreadful aims was to destroy the entire Jewish population of Europe. More than six million Jews and other peoples died in concentration camps such as this one at Buchenwald.

▼ In 1942, the German conquest of Europe reached its greatest extent. Very few countries managed to avoid the fighting.

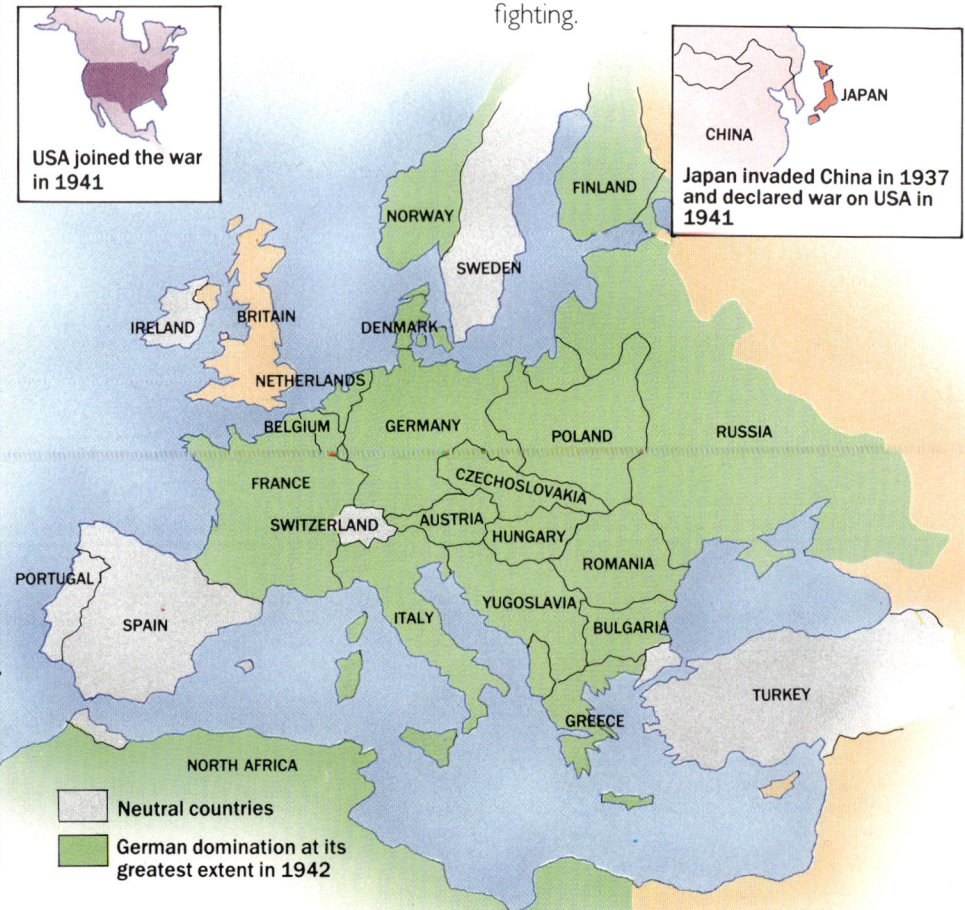

1914-1945

▲ On 6 August 1945, an atomic bomb was dropped on the Japanese city of Hiroshima. This photograph shows the terrible devastation caused by the bomb.

◀ In 1945, the American, Russian and British leaders – Franklin Roosevelt, Joseph Stalin and Winston Churchill – met at Yalta in Russia to decide how to divide up post-war Europe.

▼ After 1945, the German capital Berlin, like Germany itself, was divided into two. Conflicts arose and in 1961 the Berlin Wall was built to divide east Berlin from west. Towards the end of 1989 popular protest in East Germany led to the dismantling of the wall.

▲ In 1947, India gained independence from Britain. India became mainly Hindu, and a new State, Pakistan, was created for the Muslims. Both Burma and Ceylon (Sri Lanka) also received their freedom. There was considerable bloodshed during this partition, and the Indian leader Gandhi was assassinated.

In 1947, a Jewish homeland was created in Israel. In 1948, the Palestinian occupants of the country were defeated by the new Israeli army. Since then, three more wars have broken out between Israel and its Arab neighbours.

1914–1945

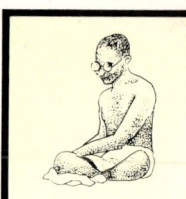

A Troubled World

The Cold War

In 1945 American troops liberated Western Europe from German control, while Russian troops had liberated Eastern Europe. Together the **superpowers** of the Soviet Union and the United States dominated Europe. But differences soon emerged between them. The Soviet Union felt threatened by the American presence in Europe, while the United States feared that the Soviet Union wanted to extend its control of Eastern Europe. By 1949, Europe was divided into two armed camps, both engaged in what was known as the Cold War.

When war broke out in Korea in 1950 and then in Vietnam in 1954, the Soviet Union and China supported one side while the United States supported the other. In other disputes too, in the Middle East, Africa and South America, the two superpowers supported opposing sides. The years from 1945 were also marked by an increasing nuclear arms race between the superpowers.

In 1985 Mikhail Gorbachev became Soviet premier and introduced a new policy of *glasnost* (openness) and *perestroika* (economic reform) in the Soviet Union. Rivalry between the two powers began to decrease as both the United States and the Soviet Union discussed the possibility of

continues on page 36

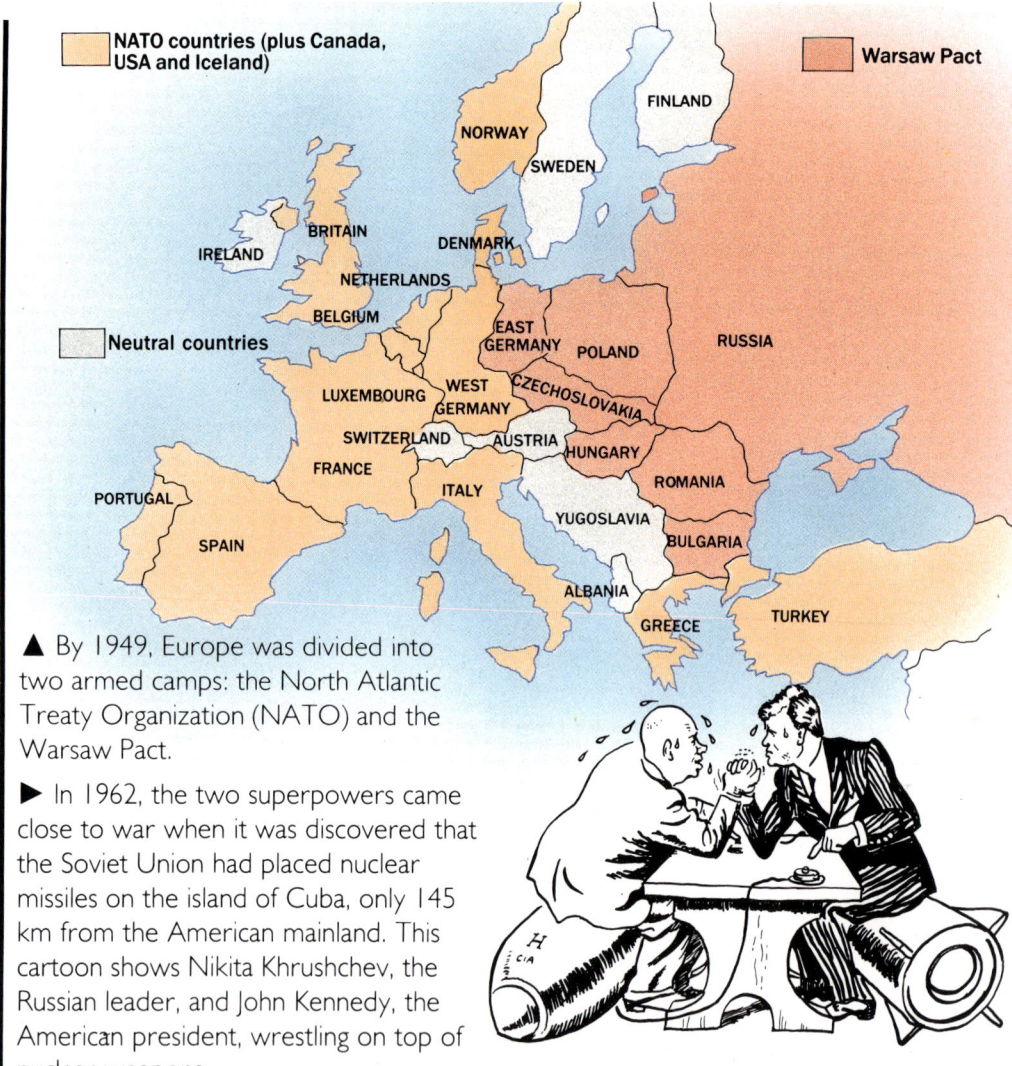

▲ By 1949, Europe was divided into two armed camps: the North Atlantic Treaty Organization (NATO) and the Warsaw Pact.

▶ In 1962, the two superpowers came close to war when it was discovered that the Soviet Union had placed nuclear missiles on the island of Cuba, only 145 km from the American mainland. This cartoon shows Nikita Khrushchev, the Russian leader, and John Kennedy, the American president, wrestling on top of nuclear weapons.

◀ In 1968 Soviet troops invaded Prague, when Czechoslovakia tried to break away from Soviet control. But by 1989 Soviet control had relaxed and popular pro-democracy movements swept through Czechoslovakia, Hungary, Romania and the rest of Eastern Europe.

1945–

◀ Superpower rivalry extended into outer space. In 1957, the Soviet Union launched the world's first satellite into orbit around the world. In 1961 the Soviet Union became the first country to put a man into space. The United States launched a series of rockets with the aim of landing people on the moon. This they achieved in 1969. In 1975, however, both countries worked together on a joint space mission.

▶ In 1969, the American astronaut Neil Armstrong (right) became the first person to land on the moon. For the first time in human history, it was possible to see our planet Earth from space (far right).

▼ Vietnamese refugees run to a helicopter to take them to safety. Between 1954 and 1975, war raged between North and South Vietnam. The Soviet Union and China supported the North, and the United States supported the South. The war cost many American and Vietnamese lives, and ended with victory for the North after America withdrew its troops in 1973.

▲ In 1987 Ronald Reagan, the American president, and Mikhail Gorbachev, the Soviet leader, signed a treaty to dismantle intermediate-range nuclear missiles. This decision was welcomed by many people who hoped that the treaty marked the first step towards complete nuclear disarmament.

nuclear disarmament. In 1989 popular uprisings in Eastern Europe also eased tension and heralded the ending of the Cold War.

China

In 1911, China became a republic after a revolt by the Kuomintang political party overthrew the Manchu emperor. However, real power did not lie with the new government but with powerful **warlords**, who ruled the many provinces of China. In 1926, the Kuomintang general, Chiang Kai-shek defeated the warlords with the help of the Chinese Communist Party. He set up a national government in the city of Nanking. Once in power, he threw the Communists out of the government and killed many of their leaders. Fighting broke out between the two sides. By 1949, the Communists, led by Mao Ze-dong, were triumphant.

The Communists under Mao set about rebuilding China. They put industry and agriculture under state control and made huge attempts to feed the 1,000 million people in the country. China allied itself with the Soviet Union and received technical aid in developing the country. But in 1960 the two governments quarrelled and the aid stopped. Since then, the Communist Party has kept the country under tight control. Dissent against the government was squashed during the Cultural Revolution between 1966 and 1969.

◀ In October 1934, the Communists decided to leave their stronghold on the coast of China and move inland. Led by Mao Ze-dong, 100,000 people set out on the Long March. They covered 60 to 100 kilometres a day and arrived at their destination a year later. Only 30,000 of the original marchers completed the 10,000-kilometre march.

▲ In order to unite the country, the Chinese leader Mao Ze-dong encouraged a cult of personality. Millions of people bought and read *The Thoughts of Chairman Mao*, his collection of sayings.

▶ In 1989, students in Beijing (Peking) and other cities requested more democracy and freedom in China. The Chinese government refused to grant these requests, and crushed the peaceful student movement with military force. Many people were killed or imprisoned.

1945–

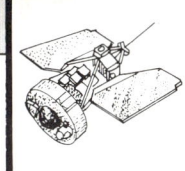

Technology and Pop Culture

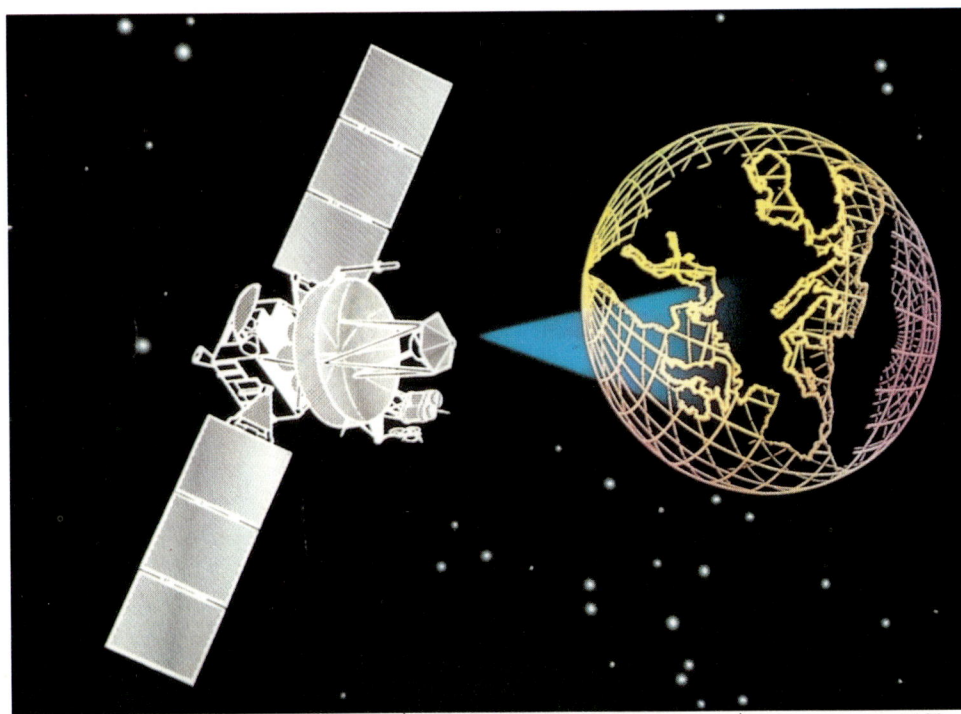

Today the regions of our world are more closely linked than ever before. It is possible to travel around the globe in hours, while satellites can broadcast events and relay messages around the globe in seconds. Television has brought every area of the world into our homes and there are few places in the world left undisturbed by tourists. As a result, differences between the various countries of the world are slowly breaking down. Computers speak their own common language to each other across the globe. Fashions in clothes, music, design and art are now universal.

▲ The first satellite was launched by the Soviet Union in 1957. Since then, thousands of satellites have been sent into orbit around the Earth.

◀ Satellite communication has brought television to the remotest parts of the world.

Pop music started in the 1950s. Groups such as the Beatles (*left*) and singers like Michael Jackson (*right*) are known in every country. Their records sell millions of copies.

37

A divided world

Since 1945 a wide gap has emerged between the rich countries of Europe, North America, Australasia and the Far East, and the poorer countries of Africa, Asia and Central and South America.

The rich countries all have highly-developed industries and economies. In Western Europe, 12 countries have joined together in a Common Market to bring their economies closer together, while in the Far East, Japan has become the richest nation in the world. In contrast, many of the poor countries have little industry and only primitive agriculture. Many of these countries only received their independence in the 1960s and 1970s when the European powers such as France and Britain began to dismantle their overseas empires. In countries such as Tanzania and Zambia, this move to independence was peaceful, but in Algeria and Mozambique, for example, there was much bloodshed. Some of these new nations are prosperous but many suffer considerable poverty made worse by famine, civil war, disease and over-population.

In order to build up their economies, many poor nations have borrowed money from the rich nations of Europe and the United States. The repayment of these loans has been expensive and has kept many of the poor nations in poverty. Today the gap between rich and poor is one of the world's most urgent problems.

▲ The conflict between Israel and its Arab neighbours has made the Middle East one of the world's most troubled areas.

◀ In 1910, South Africa became an independent nation. Since then the white minority of the population has held absolute power through a system called **apartheid** (racial segregation). Apartheid denies all rights to the majority of South Africans, who are black. Despite repression, black resistance continues. In 1990 the ban against political opposition groups was lifted and some political prisoners, such as Nelson Mandela of the African National Congress (ANC) were freed after many years in prison.

▼ In 1979, Ayatollah Khomeini became the leader of Iran. He ruled the country according to the Koran, the **Islamic** holy book. Until his death in 1989, he was the leader of a revival of Islamic fundamentalism.

1945–

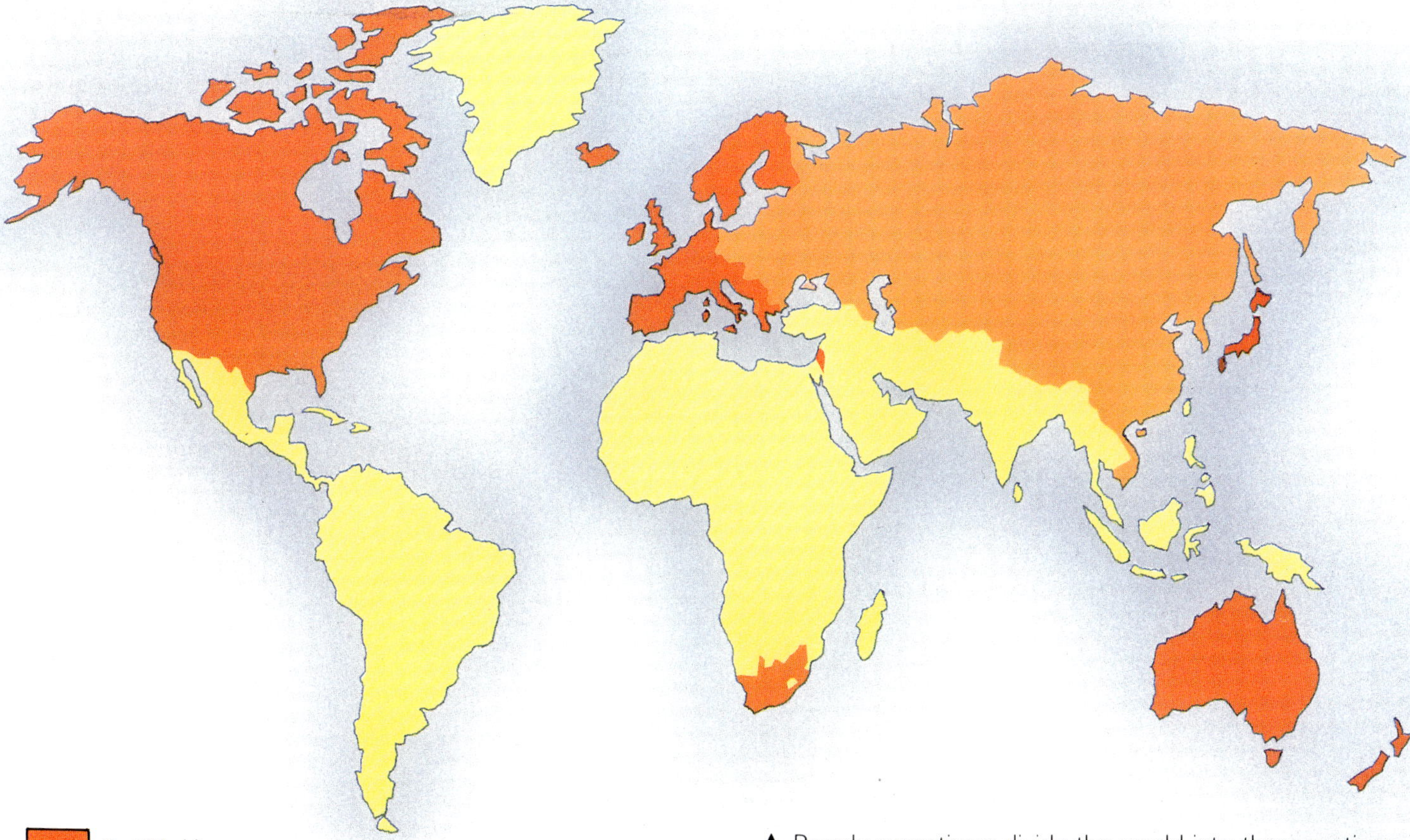

- First World
- Second World
- Third World

▲ People sometimes divide the world into three sections. The so-called First World, or 'developed market economies', contains the United States and its allies in Western Europe, the Far East and Australasia. The Second World, or 'centrally planned economies', consists of the Soviet Union, China and other communist states in Eastern Europe and Asia. The **Third World**, or 'developing market economies', includes most of Africa, Asia and South and Central America. However, many people dislike these labels because they are artificial and are based on economic wealth rather than the culture of the countries, and have been imposed by the richer countries on the poorer ones.

▼ Many parts of Africa have suffered crop failures, drought, floods and cyclones. In some countries, such as Mozambique (*below*), civil wars have led to the collapse of the national economy and food production. Such countries have become dependent for aid on Western countries.

▼ Many of the states in Central America are under the economic and political control of the United States. In 1979, a revolution in Nicaragua overthrew the American-supported ruler and replaced him with a popular government.

1945–

One world?

Over the last 200 years, the population of the world has risen — from about 600 million to more than five billion (5,000 million) in 1990. Some experts believe that by the year 2000 it will have risen to eight or ten billion. Of this huge population, two-thirds live in the Third World, in areas where poverty is so great that one in five children die before they reach their fifth birthday and most families lack decent food, housing, and medical attention.

Poverty is not the only problem facing the world today. During the 1980s, scientists have become more aware that human actions are harming our planet Earth. Industrial pollution and the exploitation of the world's natural resources are destroying irreplaceable plant and animal life and harming the delicate structure of the atmosphere. Disasters such as the industrial accident at Bhopal, in India, in which at least 2500 people were killed by poisonous gas in 1984 alerted people to the dangers of our modern world.

We are now more aware than ever that what happens in one part of the world has a direct effect on the rest of the world. This awareness has led to the formation of groups like Friends of the Earth and Greenpeace, whose aims are to protect the people, animals and plant life of our planet and ensure that future generations will be able to enjoy the world we live in today.

▼ Clearing the rainforest for the trans-American highway. Since the Second World War more than half of the world's rainforest has been cut down, destroying thousands of species of plants and animals.

▼ In 1984, a famine broke out in Ethiopia. The Irish singer Bob Geldorf arranged a huge international rock concert to raise money for the starving peoples. The Band Aid project sent food and other supplies to Ethiopia, as well as technical expertise to help the Ethiopians.

▶ Children in Oman learning about the wildlife of their country. All over the world people are becoming more aware of the need to conserve the Earth's natural resources.

Glossary

Words in this book in **bold** are explained in the Glossary below.

Alliance A friendly agreement between peoples, groups or countries.
Apartheid The policy of racial segregation pursued in South Africa.
Aristocracy The nobility or other privileged groups in a country.
Arms Race Rivalry between countries to build up supplies of weapons and weaponry.
Bourgeoisie The professional classes in society, such as teachers and lawyers.
Capitalism An economic system in which goods are produced for profit and investment is provided by a small group of people.
Civil War A war between different groups of people within one country.
Cold War Hostility between two countries that does not result in actual fighting.
Colony A settlement abroad which is ruled or governed by another country. Colonists are people who leave their home country to live in a colony.
Commerce Trade or buying or selling.
Communism An economic and political system in which the state owns all property and means of production.
Democracy Government by the people, who rule the country through an elected parliament or assembly.
Dictator An unelected head of state who rules a country by force.
Dynasty A ruling family or series of rulers from one family.
Economy The financial and commercial affairs of a country, involving the use of money.
Empire A group of countries under one ruler.
Fascism A political system in which all power is concentrated in a strong, centralized state led by a dictator.
General Strike A refusal to work by employees in every trade in one country until certain demands are met.
Independence Self-government for a colony, granted by an empire.
Islam The religion which holds that Allah is the only God and Muhammad is his prophet. Followers of Islam are called Muslims.
Monarchy A country ruled by a king or queen.
Nation A group of people under one government.
Nationalism Determination of a group of people to run their own affairs as a state or nation.
Neutral A country which refuses to take sides in international disputes or join in international military alliances.
Plantation A large estate or area of land planted with trees or one crop such as coffee, sugar, tea, cotton or tobacco.
Republic A country with an elected head of state.
Revolution A total, sometimes violent, change of political or economic conditions and their replacement with a new system.
Slavery The ownership of people as property.
Socialism A political system based on the belief that the people as a whole should own and control a country's wealth.
State A country or part of a country which governs its own affairs.
Superpower A nation that has power and influence throughout the world, based on its economic and military might.
Tax Money paid by people to a government for the administration of the country.
Technology The practical use of scientific discoveries and inventions.
Third World A term sometimes used to describe developing market economies, in particular the poor countries of Africa, Asia, and South and Central America.
Trade The process of buying and selling goods.
Warlord A military leader who governs a part of a country as if it is his own property.
World War A war fought between nations throughout the world.

Europe	**Near East**	**Africa**
1760s Industrial Revolution starts in Britain.
1762–96 Catherine the Great rules Russia.
1789 French Revolution starts.
1792 French declare republic and execute king in 1793.
1799 Napoleon takes power in France.
1815 Napoleon defeated by British at Waterloo. The French monarchy is restored.
1848 Revolutions break out across Europe.
1861–70 Italy is united.
1870 France becomes a republic.
1871 Germany is united.
1914–18 First World War.
1917 Russian Revolution.
1919 Treaty of Versailles establishes new countries in Eastern Europe.
1922 Ireland becomes independent from Britain.
1933 Hitler takes power in Germany.
1936–9 Spanish Civil War.
1939–45 Second World War.
1948 Communist governments take power in Eastern Europe.
1949 NATO and Warsaw Pact set up.
1957 Treaty of Rome establishes Common Market.
1968 Russian troops invade Czechoslovakia.
1989/90 Popular pro-democracy uprisings throughout Eastern Europe.	**1760** Ottoman Turks rule most of Near East.
1820 Britain establishes control in Persian Gulf states.
1908 Revolution in Turkey.
1914–18 First World War.
1917 Britain issues Balfour Declaration promising a Jewish homeland in Palestine.
1918 Ottoman Empire collapses: Iraq becomes independent.
1922 Turkish Republic established under Atatürk.
1922 Syria and Lebanon under French control, Palestine and Jordan under British control.
1932 Saudi Arabia united.
1939–45 Second World War.
1943 Syria and Lebanon become independent.
1946 Jordan becomes independent.
1947–8 Palestine is partitioned and the Jewish state of Israel is set up.
1948 Arab–Israeli War.
1956 Egyptian take-over of Suez Canal leads to Israeli invasion and British–French occupation of Canal.
1967 Six Day Arab–Israeli War.
1973 Yom Kippur Arab–Israeli War.
1974– Civil War in Lebanon.
1979 Peace Treaty between Egypt and Israel.
1980–88 Iran–Iraq War.	**1795** Britain acquires Cape of Good Hope from the Dutch.
1822 USA establishes Liberia as an independent state for freed slaves.
1830 France invades Algeria.
1835–7 Dutch settlers (Boers) leave Cape Colony in Great Trek inland.
1842–3 War between Boers and British.
1869 Suez Canal opened.
1880s Africa divided up by European powers.
1899–1902 Boer War between Britain and Boers.
1910 South Africa becomes independent state in British Empire.
1914–18 First World War.
1935 Italy invades Ethiopia.
1939–45 Second World War.
1954–62 Civil War in Algeria leads to French withdrawal and Algerian independence.
1957 Ghana receives its independence from Britain.
1960 French African colonies become independent.
1975 Portugal declares all its African colonies independent.
1980 Zimbabwe is the last British colony in Africa to receive its independence.
1989 Open elections in Namibia, south-west Africa.
1990 South African Government lifts ban on several opposition groups and releases some political prisoners, including Mandela.

Timeline

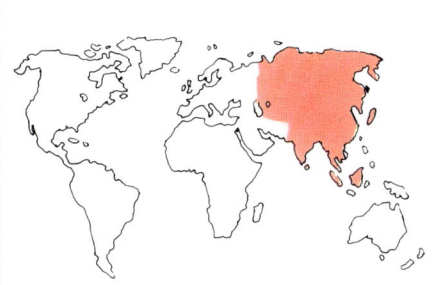

Asia

The Americas

Australasia

1763 Britain establishes control over India. **1839–42** Trade War between China and Britain. **1853** USA forces Japan to trade with foreigners. **1857–8** Indian Mutiny against British rule. **1861** France establishes first colonies in Indo-China. **1868** Japan starts to modernize itself. **1900** Boxer Rebellion against foreign influence in China. **1904–5** Russian–Japanese War; Japan controls Korea. **1911** Chinese Revolution leads to overthrow of Manchu Dynasty and establishment of republic. **1914–18** First World War. **1927** Start of Chinese Civil War between Nationalists and Communists. **1931** Japanese begin conquest of China. **1939–45** Second World War **1946–54** War against French control of Indo-China. **1947** India and Pakistan gain independence from Britain. **1949** Dutch grant independence to Indonesia. **1949** Communist Party takes control in China. **1950–3** Korean War. **1954–73** Vietnam War leads to union of Vietnam in 1975. **1989** Pro-democracy movement in Beijing, China is severely repressed.	**1763** Britain gains complete control of Canada; acquires other colonies in America. **1775–83** American Revolution. **1776** American colonies declare their independence. **1783** United States formed. **1789** George Washington is first president of USA. **1804** Haiti becomes independent after successful slave revolt. **1808–25** Spanish and Portuguese colonies in South and Central America fight for their independence. **1861–5** American Civil War. **1867** Alaska is bought by USA from Russia. **1867** Canada becomes independent from Britain. **1869** Railway link across USA. **1914** Panama Canal opens. **1917** USA declares war on Germany. **1929** Wall Street crash leads to Great Depression. **1932–45** F. D. Roosevelt becomes US president. **1941** USA enters Second World War. **1945** United Nations Organisation founded. **1963** US president John Kennedy assassinated. **1968** US Civil rights leader Martin Luther King assassinated. **1987** USA signs INF Treaty with Soviet Union.	**1768–79** Captain Cook explores the South Pacific and claims Australia for Britain. **1778** The first convicts are transported from Britain to Sydney. **1840** New Zealand becomes a British colony. **1880s** British, French and Germans colonize South Pacific. **1900** Hawaii becomes an American colony. **1901** Australia becomes an independent state in the British Empire. **1907** New Zealand becomes an independent state in the British Empire. **1914–18** First World War. **1920** Australia and Japan acquire former German colonies in the Pacific. **1927** Canberra becomes the federal capital of Australia. **1939–45** Second World War. **1941** Japanese bomb American naval base at Pearl Harbor, Hawaii, and bring USA into World War II. **1959** Hawaii becomes 50th member of the United States. **1970s** Many British island colonies in South Pacific receive their independence. **1975** Papua New Guinea receives its independence from Australia. **1985** South Pacific Forum draws up the South Pacific Nuclear Free Zone Treaty.

Timeline

Index

Page numbers in *italics* refer to illustrations

A
Africa 22–3, *22*, 38, 39
agriculture 10, *11*, 31, 39
aircraft *27*
apartheid *38*
arms race 26, *26*
Armstrong, Neil 35
atomic bombs 32, *33*
Austria 18, 26, 28, 30, 32

B
Band Aid project *40*
Bastille fortress 13
Beatles *37*
Belgium 18; colonies 22
Berlin Wall *33*
Bessemer, Henry 17
bicycles 27, *27*
Boers 23
Bolívar, Simon 15
Bolsheviks 29
Bonaparte, Joseph 15
Bonaparte, Napoleon 13, 14, *14*, 15
Boston Tea Party *12*
'Boxer' rebellion *24*
Britain: colonies/Empire 8, *8–9*, 12, 14, 20, 22, 23, 31; industry 10–11, 16–17; reform *18*; World Wars 28, 32
Burma 32, 33

C
canals 10
Canton *24*
Caribbean 8, 15
Catherine the Great *9*
Cavour, Count 18
Central America 8, *15*, 39
Chartists *18*
Chiang Kai-shek 36
child labour 10, *17*
China 8, 18, 24, 32, 34; Communists 36, *36*
coal 10, 11, 16, *16*
Common Market 38
Communists 18, 29, 36, *36*
concentration camps *32*
Crystal Palace (London) *17*
Cuba crisis 34
Cultural Revolution (China) 36
Curie, Marie *19*
Custer, General George 21
Czechoslovakia 32, 34

D
Daguerre, Louis 19
Darwin, Charles 19, *19*
Declaration of Independence *12*

E
East Indiaman (ship) *9*
Ethiopia 22, 40
Europe: colonies 8, *8–9*, 20, 22; Industrial Revolution 10, 16, 22; Napoleon 14; revolutions (1848) *18*; alliances 26; World Wars 28, *28*, 32, *32–3*; Cold War 34; Common Market 38, *see also under names of individual states*
evolution, theory of 19

F
factories 10, 11, 16, *28*
farming 10, *11*, 31, 39
fascism 31
films *30*
Ford, Henry 27
France: colonies 8, 12, 14, 20, 22, *24*; Revolution/Napoleonic era 13–15, *14*, 18; World Wars 28, 32
Franco, General Francisco 31
Freud, Sigmund 19, *19*

G
Gandhi, Mahatma *31*, 33
Germany: industry 16, *17*, 26; nationalism 18; colonies *22*, 24, 28; World Wars 28, 32; between wars 30, 31
Gorbachev, Mikhail 34, *35*
Goya, Francisco 15
Great Depression (USA) 30, *30*, 31
Great Exhibition (1851) *17*
Greece 18
guillotines *13*

H
Haiti 15
Hargreaves, James 11
Hiroshima 32, *33*
Hitler, Adolf 30, *31*, 32
Holland *see* Netherlands
Hungary 18, 34

I
India 22, *23*, *31*, 33
Indians, American 20, *21*
Industrial Revolution 10–11, 16, 22
Iran 38
Ireland 26
Islam 38
Israel 33, *33*, 38
Italy 18, *22*, 24, 32

J
Jackson, Michael *37*
Japan 8, 16, 24, *25*, 38; World Wars 32
Jefferson, Thomas 12

K
Kennedy, John 34
Khomeini, Ayatollah 38
Khrushchev, Nikita 34
Kingsley, Mary 22
Kollontai, Alexandra 29
Korea 24, 34

L
League of Nations 30
Lenin, V.I. 29, *29*
Leningrad 29
Lister, Joseph 19
Long March, the (China) 36
Louis XIV, King of France 13
Louisiana Purchase 20, *20*
Luddites *11*

M
Mandela, Nelson 38
Mao Ze-dong 36, *36*
Marx, Karl 18
medicine 19
mining 16, *16*, 23
moon-landing *35*
motor cars 27, *27*
Mozambique 38, *39*

N
Napoleon Bonaparte 13, 14, *14*, 15
Netherlands 18; colonies 8, *9*, 23
Newcomen, Thomas 11
New Deal, the (USA) 30

New Zealand 22, 26
Nicaragua *39*
Nicholas II, Tsar 29
North Atlantic Treaty Organization (NATO) *34*
nuclear power 19
nuclear weapons 32, *33*, 34, 35

O
Oman *40*

P
Pakistan 33
Paris 10, *13*
Pasteur, Louis 19, *19*
Pearl Harbor attack 32
Peking (Beijing) *9*, *36*
Perry, Matthew *25*
photography *19*, *30*
Poland 30, 32
pollution, industrial *40*
pop culture 37
population growth 10, 40
Portugal 8, 22, 24
Prague *34*
Prussia 18

R
railways 16, *20*, 22, *25*, *27*
Reagan, Ronald *35*
refrigerator ships *27*
Rhodes, Cecil 22
Robespierre, Maximilien 13
Romania, 30, 34
Roosevelt, Franklin D. 30, *33*
Ruhr industry *17*
Russia: Russian Empire 8, *9*, *20*, *24*; industry 16; revolutions 18, 26, 28, 29, *29*, *see also* Soviet Union

S
San Martin, José de 15
satellite communication 37, *37*
Serbia 28
Sitting Bull, Chief *21*
slavery *8*, 15, 21, 23
slums *17*
South Africa *see* Africa
South America 8, *15*, 18
Soviet Union 32, 34, *35*, 36, *see also* Russia
space exploration 35, *35*
Spain 8, *15*, 20, 24; Civil War 31
spinning jenny *11*

Sri Lanka (Ceylon) 33
Stalin, Joseph 29, *33*
steam power *11*
steel industry 16, *17*
Suez Canal 23

T
technology 37
textiles 10, *11*, *16*, *17*
Third World *39*, 40
tourism 27
Toussaint L'Ouverture, Pierre *15*
trench warfare *28*
Tubman, Harriet *21*
Turkey 18, 28; Ottoman Empire 8, *9*

U
United States of America: the 13 colonies 8, *8*, 14; formed 12; industry 16; growth of 20–1, *21*; colonies 24, *25*; World Wars 28, 32; Great Depression 30; Cold War 34, 36; space exploration 35

V
Vendée, the, revolt in (France) 13
Versailles, Treaty of (1919) 30
Vienna settlement (1815) 18
Vietnam 34, *35*

W
Wall Street crash *30*
Warsaw Pact 34
Washington, George 12
water power 10, *11*
Watt, James 11
welfare, social 26, 30
women 10, *16*, *28*, 29; French Revolution *13*; votes for 26, *26*
Wright brothers *27*

Y
Yalta Conference (1945) *33*

Z
Zeppelin airships *27*

Acknowledgements

The publishers wish to thank the following for supplying photographs for this book:

Page 11 Mary Evans Picture Library (middle) The Hulton-Deutsch Collection (bottom right); 12 The British Library (top) Peter Newark's Pictures (bottom); 13 Mary Evans Picture Library; 14 The Bridgeman Art Library; 15 The Bridgeman Art Library (left) Mary Evans Picture Library (right); 16 The Mansell Collection; 17 Ann Ronan Picture Library (left) Mary Evans Picture Library (right) Grisewood & Dempsey Ltd (bottom); 18 The Hulton-Deutsch Collection; 19 Mary Evans Picture Library (left) The Bettman Archive (right) The Hulton-Deutsch Collection (bottom); 20 The Library of Congress; 21 The Hulton-Deutsch Collection; 22 Punch Library; 23 The Hulton-Deutsch Collection (top) Mary Evans Picture Library (bottom); 24 The Mansell Collection (top) Mary Evans Picture Library (bottom); 25 The Hulton-Deutsch Collection (top) Courtesy, Kyoto Costume Institute (bottom); 26 Mary Evans Picture Library; 27 Mary Evans Picture Library (left) The Mansell Collection (right); 28 The Imperial War Museum; 29 Novosti (top) The David King Collection (bottom); 30 The Kobal Collection (top) The Hulton-Deutsch Collection (bottom); 31 The Hulton-Deutsch Collection (top) Camera Press (left) Peter Newark's Pictures (right); 32 The Imperial War Museum; 33 Camera Press; 34 Camera Press; 35 Society for Cultural Relations with U.S.S.R. (top) NASA (middle left) NRSC Library (middle right) The Hutchison Library (bottom left) Associated Press (bottom right); 36 The David King Collection (top) Associated Press (bottom); 37 ZEFA (top) The Hutchison Library (middle) Popperfoto (bottom left) Associated Press (bottom right); 38 Associated Press; 39 Associated Press (left) The Hutchison Library (right); 40 The Hutchison Library (top) Band Aid (middle) ICCE Photolibrary/Mark Boulton (bottom).

Front cover: The Bridgeman Art Library (top) ZEFA (bottom)
Back cover: Peter Newark's Pictures

Endpapers: NRSC Library